Foundations of the
Fourth Turning of Hasidism

A Manifesto

Foundations of the Fourth Turning of Hasidism

A MANIFESTO

Netanel Miles-Yépez
Zalman Schachter-Shalomi

Albion
Andalus

Boulder, Colorado

2014

*"The old shall be renewed,
and the new shall be made holy."*
— Rabbi Avraham Yitzhak Kook

Albion-Andalus, Inc.
P. O. Box 19852
Boulder, CO 80308
www.albionandalus.com

Design and layout by Albion-Andalus Books
Cover design by Daryl McCool
India ink illustrations by Netanel Miles-Yépez
Cover illustrations by Netanel Miles-Yépez
Photo of the authors by Don Murray.

ISBN-13: 978-0692238301 (Albion-Andalus Books)
ISBN-10: 0692238301

For
Hillel Zeitlin

And with gratitude to
Helena Foster

A Call for a New Hasidism

Hasidism in Poland has to return if it does not want to die (and it must not die, for "thought that proceeds from sublime Wisdom is not to be destroyed"). It must return to the Ba'al Shem Tov and his disciples, those bearers of divine compassion. Hasidism needs to be restored to its source. Then it will nourish the spirit and soul of all humanity . . .

The holy Hasidic word needs to be carried far, far beyond the boundaries of Poland, even beyond the bounds of the entire Jewish people. The inner power of this word needs to call forth to all humanity, arousing them to true love, true justice, and the true "kingdom of heaven."

— Hillel Zeitlin, Warsaw, Poland, 1916-1917
(translated by Arthur Green)

HASIDISM

HASIDISM is a movement of the spirit that arises in us as a yearning for God and the sacred, and which expresses itself through acts of loving-kindness and service to the same. Hasidism is the willingness to make ourselves transparent to God's grace and will, to live in the authentic Presence of God—*nokhaḥ p'nai Ha'Shem*—as if facing God in every moment, allowing this awareness to change our behavior, to make sacred acts out of potentially profane and purely secular moments.

This movement of the spirit, at the core of the Hasidic tradition, is also a universal impulse, as is the attitude of active-receptivity to the divine which it fosters. Thus, what has been called 'Hasidism' over the centuries is only the story of the evolution and manifestation of that universal impulse and attitude among the Jewish people—for whom it has become a communal *ethos*, wedded to the primary revelation of Judaism, to the Jewish myth and *magisterium*—with unique characteristics and experiential outcomes.

From this perspective, Hasidism is both the origin and fulfillment of Judaism's spiritual potential, arising and developing in different periods to meet the unique needs of a specific time and place. Through the millennia, Judaism has witnessed the emergence of numerous Hasidic movements, both large and small, some bearing the name, and others not. Among the former are four significant Hasidic movements which represent the Hasidic ideal as it existed in three different paradigms and historical periods: the classical period of Greco-Roman Palestine; the medieval period of Muslim Egypt and Christian Germany; and the pre-industrial period of Eastern Europe and Russia.

We call these movements, 'turnings,' literally, revolutions that demonstrate the adaptation of the Hasidic tradition to a particular time and place.[1] Judaism, as we have already suggested, has seen three such turnings of Hasidism (in four separate movements), each an appropriate expression of the highest and most integrated levels of spirituality available in that period, which is to say, informed by the spirit of the times and influenced by the chthonic element of the place.[2]

The First Turning of Hasidism

In the Mishnah, we are told about the Ḥasidim ha'Rishonim, the 'First Hasidism.' Although this expression is likely a general reference to the 'pious of times past,' the examples given of their actions are consistent with what we know of Hasidism in other periods.[3] Moreover, in the classical period of Greco-Roman Palestine, we find references to a Jewish sect known as the *asidaioi* or *essaioi* in Greek, which may be the first actual community to be called Ḥasidim, as these words are generally believed to be Hellenized versions of Hebrew and Aramaic originals (most likely, *ḥasidei* or *ḥasya*, both meaning, 'pious').[4] In the Book of Maccabees, they are called, "stalwarts of Israel, devoted in the cause of the Law."[5] And in the writings of Philo of Alexandria, it is said that they are "above all, devoted to the service of God" and seek "a freedom which can never be enslaved."[6] It is generally accepted that these Ḥasidim (usually called Essenes, based on their Latin name, *esseni)*[7] are the authors of the Dead Sea Scrolls and the sect whose practices and beliefs are described therein.

THE SECOND TURNING OF HASIDISM

The Second Turning of Hasidism is best seen in two movements of the medieval period, emerging independently in separate geographic areas and cultural climates which clearly influenced the particular expression of Hasidism in those places. These were the Ḥasidei Ashkenaz in Christian Germany, and the Ḥasidei Sefarad in Muslim Egypt.[8] The Ḥasidei Ashkenaz were led by the famous Kalonymous family of kabbalists (most notably, Rabbi Yehudah He'Ḥasid, the author of the *Sefer Ḥasidim*) who practiced an almost monastic form of Hasidism. The Ḥasidei Ashkenaz planted seeds in Europe that would spring up in many smaller Hasidic movements in the centuries that followed. Similarly, the Ḥasidei Sefarad were led by the philosopher-mystics of the Maimuni family (most notably, Rabbi Avraham Maimuni of Fustat, the son of Maimonides, and the author of the *Kifayat al-Abidin*) who forged a community of Hasidic contemplatives whose teachings and practices paralleled those of Muslim Sufis, whom they openly admired.

THE THIRD TURNING OF HASIDISM

The Third Turning of Hasidism flowered in the pre-industrial period of Eastern Europe and Russia under the leadership of Rabbi Yisrael ben Eliezer, called the Ba'al Shem Tov, and his successor, Rabbi Dov Baer, the Maggid of Mezritch, whose lives and teachings set the pattern of Hasidism for centuries to come, even into our own day. Integrating and building on the spiritual work of previous Hasidic movements like the Ḥasidei Ashkenaz, as well as generations of kabbalistic endeavor, Hasidism exploded with creativity in the 18th-century. Its approach was characterized by a new embrace of the material world as a divine manifestation, by an acceptance and celebration of the potential of the common Jew, by a joyous engagement with life, by prayer and contemplation of extraordinary depth, as well as stories and teachings that turned conventional thinking upside down. Owing to its positive approach and popular appeal, the movement spread like wildfire over Eastern Europe and Russia, making it the most influential of the three Hasidic movements.

The Fourth Turning of Hasidism

With the emergence of a global consciousness in the 20th-century, perhaps best articulated in the work of the philosopher, Pierre Teilhard de Chardin, and symbolized by the first images of our planet as seen from outer space, the paradigm of every known religion began to shift irrevocably. Before the dawning of this global consciousness, every religious tradition followed a more or less independent trajectory, or could at least maintain the illusion of doing so. But once the 'shape and sharing of the planet' was known, all trajectories began to align, causing upheaval in every religious tradition and spiritual lineage. Thus, a global consciousness is both the primary catalyst for, and the defining characteristic of the Fourth Turning of Hasidism.

The following are common elements shared by all the previous turnings of Hasidism in the view of the Fourth Turning:

Repentance

The beginning and end of a Hasid's spiritual path is *t'shuvah,* continually 'turning' one's awareness back to the divine source, remembering from whence we come and our common identity in the divine being. *T'shuvah* is also repentance, a reorientation to a radical humility that serves as the foundation for true righteousness in our world. No matter how righteous one appears or feels oneself to be, there is always room for repentance; for the paradox of true righteousness is the requirement of self-abasement, realizing one's utter inability to serve God perfectly and humbling oneself in response.[9]

PROPHECY

Nevertheless, the primary goal of Hasidism is a direct connection to God, often characterized as *nevu'ah*, 'prophecy,' or *ru'ah ha'kodesh*, the 'spirit of holiness.' Hasidism believes that the prophetic consciousness is still available (though the Sages declared the prophetic period closed at the time of the closing of the canon).[10] If Hasidism, as we have said, is a genuine 'openness to the divine will,' then prophecy is the product of such openness (as seen in the root of the word, *navi*, 'open' or 'hollow').[11] This suggests both the method and the means that allow for prophecy, or as we might characterize it today, deep intuition.

PRAYER

The primary means of cultivating one's 'openness to the divine will' is prayer, which is central to Hasidic life. In the Hasidism of the Ba'al Shem Tov, prayer is generally spoken of as *avodat Ha'Shem* or *davvenen*, 'divine service' or 'prayer in which one is deeply connected to God.'[12] In the Fourth Turning, we are also inclined to emphasize what we call 'davvenology,' the investigation of the inner process of prayer, including all aspects of worship and the Jewish liturgical life. Today, it is not enough to be able to connect in prayer; we must also understand the sacred technology which allows us to make the connection.

PRACTICES

Nevertheless, Hasidism has always embraced a variety of supererogatory methods or *hanhagot*, 'spiritual practices' that are not required in Judaism, but which are taken on by the Hasid to continue the process of making oneself transparent to God's grace and will, and to facilitate an awareness of living in the authentic Presence of God. Such *hanhagot* were often given in the form of traditional and intuitive *eitzot* or 'prescriptions,' to remedy particular spiritual maladies and to promote particular spiritual effects.[13]

GUIDANCE

Spiritual prescriptions and guidance in the ways of Hasidism are given by one's *rebbe*, a *neshamah klalit* or 'general soul' who is able to locate and connect with the souls of individual Ḥasidim because they are part of the same 'soul-cluster,' allowing for relationships of deep spiritual intimacy. The *rebbe* gives his or her guidance to the Ḥasid in the private encounter, *yeḥidut*, and in public gatherings, *farbrengen*. In the past, the person serving others as *rebbe* was often indistinguishable from the '*rebbe*-function' they performed. But in the Fourth Turning, it is recognized that the *rebbe*, though 'called to service' and to function as a *neshamah klalit* through the cultivation of their own spiritual attunement, is nevertheless, not identical with that service and function. For the projection of such a static identity limits the rebbe's personal freedom, creates unrealistic and unhelpful expectations, and allows the Ḥasid to yield personal responsibility in a way that is not conducive to spiritual growth.

Because the ability to function as a *rebbe* is rare, requiring particular spiritual gifts and a significant cultivation of them, Hasidism also recognizes the need for the *mashpiyya*, the mentor or guide, as well as the *ḥaver*, the spiritual friend. The former is an individual who has achieved maturity on the spiritual path and is thus able to help others in negotiating many of its paths and pitfalls. Likewise, friends who share the same spiritual values, and with whom one can share the journey, are also critically important.[14]

Community

The communal context for spiritual growth in Hasidism is the *farbrengen*, literally 'time spent together.' The Hasidic gathering may take place on *Shabbat*, other *yom tovim*, or at any other time of the year. Likewise, it may be led by the *rebbe* or a *mashpiyya*, or simply be a gathering of *ḥaverim*. It is a time for spiritual guidance, cultivating both joy and introspection, during which meditations and Hasidic *niggunim* are used for tuning consciousness to the right frequency for receiving Torah, and where Hasidic *ma'asiot* and *meshalim*, stories and parables, open the heart and imagination to the possibilities of living a more virtuous reality.

Law

The norms of Hasidic life and behavior are oriented around a radical engagement with Jewish law, or *halakhah*. Contrary to some modern misconceptions, Hasidism is not anti-legal and has never been casual about *halakhah*. On the contrary, Hasidism stresses the most integral, elevated, and meaningful application of every aspect of Jewish law and tradition to Jewish life. This is also the view of the Fourth Turning, which seeks to engage and examine every law and tradition, taking the needs of the time, the place, and the people into consideration, looking at the original function of the law in its original context to see how it may be best applied today to achieve similar ends.

Providence

Finally, the view of Hasidism is providential. In each turning, Hasidism has embraced an idea of providence in keeping with its own experience of divinity, as well as an awareness of the 'miraculous order' in creation. The holy Ba'al Shem Tov spoke of *hashgaḥah pratit*, a 'specific personal providence,' in which all events are seen as happening with a specific or particular purpose, beyond appearances of 'good' or 'evil.'[15] This is in keeping with his pantheistic worldview, wherein there is nothing in existence but divinity; therefore, nothing happens that is not divine or divinely ordained (however we may judge it according to our limited vision). Our own understanding of 'organismic pantheism' is but an extension of this view, merely acknowledging the dynamic and sophisticated organizing principle of ecological systems within the whole of possibility, always serving the Greater Purpose.

In one form or another, these elements have been present in every turning of Hasidism. And yet, each turning always contributes something new—new interpretations, new teachings, new practices and new ideas. The following are some of the new ideas on which the Fourth Turning bases itself:

Renewal

More than ever before, Hasidism needs to maintain an awareness of its own evolution (of which the various turnings are evidence) in the context of the greater evolution of spiritual traditions on the planet. As consciousness evolves over time and the world changes, traditions must reclaim their primary teleological impulse in order to adapt to the needs of the evolving consciousness. This process of unfolding within and adapting without, we call 'renewal.'[16] Renewal itself is characterized by the struggle to marry the *magisterium* of a religious tradition, i.e., its inherited body of knowledge and wisdom, to a new reality map or paradigmatic understanding of the universe. On a small scale, renewal is happening continuously; but it is also a process that we witness on a larger scale in certain epochs or axial moments in history, like ours, when religions and religious forms are breaking down and slowly re-organizing and re-forming over time.

An awareness of this process can help to keep our current religions and spiritual traditions healthy. For as we engage and become aware of the process of renewal, we must re-evaluate our traditional spiritual teachings and practices, considering their 'deep structures,' analyzing their function in different historical periods to better understand how they might apply, or be adapted for use in our own time.[17] This new understanding and adaptation allows us to utilize the maximum of our historical traditions, without at the same time turning a blind eye to the true needs of the present.

DEEP ECUMENISM

However, as we explore the deep structures of our own traditions, revealing the basic functionality beneath the specific wrappings, we cannot ignore their similarity to those of every other religious and spiritual tradition on the planet. Providence, as well as our own evolutionary perspective, demands that we acknowledge a similar sacred purpose at work in these deep structures, that we learn how others use them for the fulfillment of the Greater Purpose, and how others can aid us in understanding our own use of them.

While dialogue with other religious traditions undoubtedly took place in our past, it had no legitimizing basis or support in the tradition, and could rarely take place openly. Today, it is nevertheless embraced by many Jewish leaders, being seen as a salutary attempt to achieve a measure of understanding between religions, discerning similarities and differences through dialogue and close observation. However, the Ḥasid must go beyond such surface knowledge, seeking the spirit beneath the external forms and teachings, undertaking the more intrepid exploration of 'deep ecumenism,' in which one learns about *oneself* through participatory engagement with another religion or tradition.[18]

Judaism can no longer afford to see itself as the only valid religious tradition, or even as the most important. For such a view is ultimately self-defeating and destructive to the ecological system of the planet, which prefers diversity and depends on it for its own health. From this ecological perspective, every religion is like a vital organ of the planet; and for the planet's sake, each must remain healthy, functioning well in concert with the others for the health of the greater body. Thus, Jews must be the best and healthiest Jews they can be, doing their part in the planetary eco-system; but they must also do it in a way that recognizes the contributions of other religions and supports their healthy functioning.

EGALITARIANISM

As we embrace this larger 'organismic view,' seeing Judaism as a contributor to the health of the planetary system, we must not, as we have already said, forget to support the health and diversity of the internal Jewish ecological system. Judaism has, for too long, excluded women from full participation in the religious life of the community, denied the basic rights of individuals who are lesbian, gay, bisexual or transgendered, and erected high walls to protect Judaism from so-called 'outsiders.' Although there may have been times in our history when the exclusion of these groups served to preserve a fragile social order or seemed less important amid greater concerns for health and safety, today, their exclusion is untenable and acts like a cancer in the body of Judaism. If Judaism would be healed and give its most healthy functioning back to the planet, it must embrace all of these groups. And in doing so, it will find that much of its new vitality and creativity will come directly from them.

CONCLUSION

But all of this is just a beginning. It is not definitive, not the final word, nor the only view of the matter. Our words are not 'the word' of the Fourth Turning of Hasidism. They are merely the product of a longing to serve God as deeply as our Hasidic ancestors once did, recognizing the needs of our time and attempting to call the future into the present with a name. It is only Hasidism itself—i.e., making ourselves transparent to God's grace and will, and living in the authentic Presence of God—that can do the rest.

  — N.M-Y. & Z.S-S.

The Thirteen Aspirations of Faith

I.

My God,
I aspire to
Perfect faith
In Your
Infinite Light,
Issuing from the Source
Beyond time and space,
Who, longing for
A dwelling-place
In the Worlds below,
Compassionately contracts
Her Radiant Glory
In order to emanate,
Create, form, and effect
All that exists in
The Universe.

II.

My God,
I aspire to
Perfect faith
In Your Oneness
With all of creation;
A Oneness
Without a second,
A Oneness that says,
All that exists
In the Universe
Is called into being
According to
Your Desire
In every
Moment.

III.

My God,
I aspire to
Perfect faith
In Your intent
And purpose
In Creation;
That the Divine He
May become
Known to us
Through Creation,
The Divine She;
That we expand
This awareness
Until the Worlds
Are filled with the
Consciousness of God,
As the waters
Cover the sea.

IV.

My God,
I aspire to
Perfect faith
In Your unfolding plan,
In which all of us
May come to constitute
One consciously
Interconnected
And organic whole;
That every living being
May know that You
Are the One
Who constantly causes
Their existence.

V.

My God,
I aspire to
Perfect faith
In all the paths
Through which the
Holy Spirit manifests
And reveals to us;
That all Your
Manifestations are one,
Though called
By different names
Through time
And space.

VI.

My God,
I aspire to
Perfect faith
In the mission
Of each path
As an organ of
The collective being
That comprises
All existence;
That through
Your compassion
On all creatures
It be revealed to all
How integral
Each Message is
To the health
Of all the species
Of our collective
Being.

VII.

My God,
I aspire to
Perfect faith
In the reciprocity
Of Your Universe,
Which takes our
Impressions;
That everyone
Who does good
With one's own life
Takes part in the fixing
Of the world,
And that everyone
Who uses that life
For negative purposes,
Likewise participates
In the destruction
Of the world;
That every action
Has an impact
On the rest of
Existence.

VIII.

My God,
I aspire to
Perfect faith
In Your perfect
Judgment;
That the amount
Of good
In the Universe
Is greater than
The amount
Of negativity;
And that our
Entire movement
Through the chain
Of evolution
Is designed
To bring about
The fulfillment
Of Your Divine
Intention.

IX.

My God,
I aspire to
Perfect faith
In Your tradition;
That the deeds
Of our mothers
And fathers
Inure to the benefit
Of their children;
That the traditions
Passed on
Contain within them
The seeds of the light
Of Redemption.

X.

My God,
I aspire to
Perfect faith
In Your compassion;
That our prayers
Are heard and
Answered.

XI.

My God,
I aspire to
Perfect faith
In Your Holy
Presence,
Dwelling in
Our midst;
That all who
Show kindness
To living creatures
Also show kindness
To You.

XII.

My God,
I aspire to
Perfect faith
In Your continuity;
That physical death
Does not terminate
The existence
Of the soul;
That there are
Innumerable Worlds
In which souls
Reside.

XIII.

My God,
I aspire to
Perfect faith
In the fixing
Of the World;
And our part
In its awakening,
Possessing life,
Consciousness
And feeling,
Becoming a fitting
Vessel for the
Revelation of the
Divine Will.

NOTES

1. In speaking of 'turnings,' we are consciously borrowing language from the Buddhist tradition, which speaks of 'three turnings of the wheel of dharma,' describing three phases of how the wisdom of that tradition was presented according to the needs of different eras.

2. Chthonic (from the Greek word, *chthon* or 'earth') referring to how the land itself, or the landscape of a place influences expression in that place.

3. The expression *hasidim ha'rishonim* may be read both ways. It occurs many times in the Mishnah. One example is found in Berakhot 5:1.

4. Another possibility is the Aramaic word, *asyah*, 'healing.'

5. 1 Maccabees 2:42.

6. Philo of Alexandria, *Quod Omnis Probus Liber Sit*, sections XII and XIII.

7. As they are called by Pliny the Elder.

8. Although this group did identify themselves as Ḥasidim, "Hasidei Sefarad" is simply a name we have applied to them for the purpose of differentiating them from their northern siblings, the Ḥasidei Ashkenaz.

9. See Zalman Schachter-Shalomi and Netanel Miles-Yépez, *A Heart Afire: Stories and Teachings of the Early Hasidic Masters*, Philadelphia: Jewish Publication Society, 2009: 44-54, and 294-95.

10. See Ibid., 180-92.

11. From the tri-literal Hebrew root, *Nun-Beit-Beit*, which may be interpreted as 'hollow.'

12. *Davvenen* may be derived from the Latin word, *divinum,* meaning, 'divine work.'

13. See Schachter-Shalomi and Miles-Yépez, *A Heart Afire,* 306-31.

14. See Zalman Schachter-Shalomi and Netanel Miles-Yépez, *A Hidden Light: Stories and Teachings of Early HaBaD and Bratzlav Hasidism*, Santa Fe: Gaon Books, 2011: 160.

15. See Schachter-Shalomi and Miles-Yépez, *A Heart Afire,* 26-44.

16. Another term for what we have sometimes called 'paradigm shift,' a phrase originally introduced by the philosopher of science, Thomas Kuhn.

17. We have borrowed the term, 'deep structures' from Noam Chomsky's discussion of transformational grammar.

18. 'Deep ecumenism' is a phrase coined by Father Matthew Fox. Ecumenism, from the Greek, *oikoumenikos,* 'from the whole world,' originally referred to cooperative efforts between different parts of the Christian Church.

Netanel Miles-Yépez was born in Battle Creek, Michigan in 1972, and is descended from a Sefardi family of crypto-Jews. He studied History of Religions at Michigan State University and Contemplative Religion at Naropa University. Today, he is a scholar of comparative religion, a Sufi *murshid,* and co-founder of the Inayati-Maimuni Tariqat which fuses Sufi and Hasidic principles of spirituality. He currently teaches in the Department of Religious Studies at Naropa University.

Zalman Schachter-Shalomi was born in Zholkiew, Poland in 1924. Descended from a distinguished family of Belzer Hasidim, he was ordained by Habad-Lubavitch in 1947, and became one of the Sixth Lubavitcher Rebbe's first outreach workers. He earned his MA from Boston University and his DHL from Hebrew Union College. He is professor emeritus of Psychology of Religion and Jewish Mysticism at Temple University and World Wisdom Chair holder emeritus at Naropa University. Today, he is widely known as the father of the Jewish Renewal movement, and considered one of the world's foremost authorities on Hasidism and Kabbalah.

Made in the USA
Monee, IL
08 July 2026